Story Link®
Program

City
Green

Poems and Pictures by
ELEANOR SCHICK

MACMILLAN PUBLISHING CO., INC.
New York
COLLIER MACMILLAN PUBLISHERS
London

Macmillan Publishing Co., Inc.,
866 Third Avenue, New York, N.Y. 10022
Collier-Macmillan Canada Ltd.

Library of Congress catalog card number: 73-8574

Printed in the United States of America

10   9   8   7   6   5   4   3   2   1

The pictures were drawn in pencil, with an overlay for
the second color. The typeface is Caledonia, with the
display set in photo Zoppo.

Library of Congress Cataloging in Publication Data

Schick, Eleanor, date
     City green.

    1. City and town life—Juvenile poetry.   [1. City
and town life—Poetry]   I. Title.   PZ8.3.S34Ci
811'.5'4   73-8574   ISBN 0-02-781170-0

FOR LAURA AND DAVID

There is a gush of water
rushing down the street
from a fire hydrant.

It's a river
running to the ocean,
and I'm a river bird.

I would love you
if you were mine.

I would love you
if you weren't mine.

I still love you
even though
you aren't mine.

There's a baby sucking
like the whole world
was in that pacifier.

Sucking with his fingers,
and his toes, and his
eyes . . . .

His mother will be
coming soon.

9

My father is a pickup truck.
My mother is a bus.
And my little brother David
is a red fire engine
screaming his siren
down the middle of the street,
and all the cars
have to get out of his way.

Sometimes I
hear a sound
and then
the thing that
made the sound
isn't there
anymore.

I like to go
traveling on trains,
because I like the sound
of the train singing
on the train tracks.

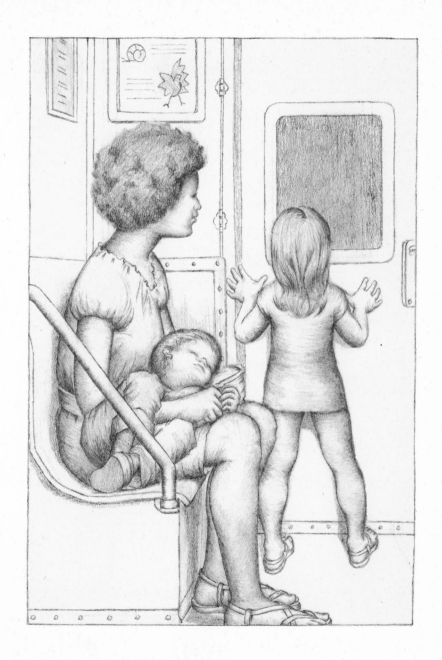

I like
summertime
because the
sun shines
through the
cracks between
the leaves,
onto
people's clothes,
and on
the grass.

David says
that since he
made his bed
this morning,
there's a
train track
in his blankets.

Before,
when I looked,
I only saw
that it was
wrinkled.

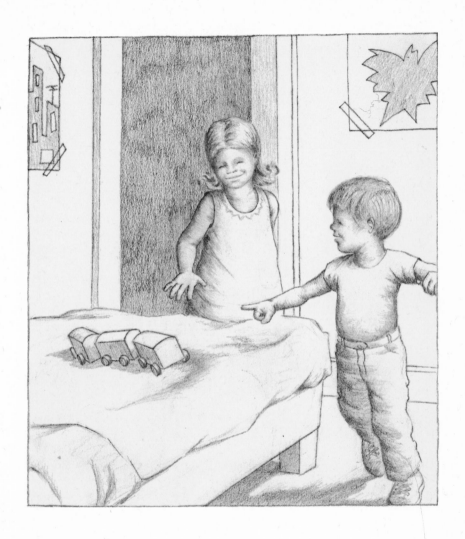

19

David said,
"I'm growing
faster than
the light switch,
so by next year
I'll be as
tall as it is."

21

I'm stupid, I'm stupid, I'm
stupid, because I
didn't laugh when
they laughed, because
the joke wasn't
funny, and
Jaimie was
hurting inside, and
I'm stupid, I'm stupid, I'm
stupid, because they
all laughed at
me, and even
Jaimie did.

The ants crawl
over my arm
and back
into the grass
again.

They mean me
no harm.

I am only a
mountain
to them.

My mother said,
"Turn around and
I'll zip your dress."

So I turned around
and around
and around
and around
and around....

I saw a little boy
walking on a wall
who walked on a wall
like David.

And he slid down
by turning around
and going on his tummy
like David.

But he didn't have
David's face.

And anyway,
David was upstairs
taking a nap.

David said
that
he
didn't want
an
Ice
Cream
Sundae,
because he
wanted
it
now.

Sometimes I make up songs
to the rhythm of the swing swinging,
and the creak of the chain creaking.

They just come to me.
I don't know how, and
I don't know why.

I make up songs, and I
sing them to myself, and
to the wind.

David and I
think that
the waves of the ocean
are the
water breathing.

My mother asked me
if I wanted
another glass of milk.

I said, "No,
I'll use
this one again...."

The sky is
evening blue and

the buildings are
brown-pink

and the windows
are like

golden sparkles
sprinkled everywhere.

39